Different Shapes, Equal Pieces

FRACTIONS AND AREA

T E R C

Investigations in Number, Data, and Space®

Dale Seymour Publications®

Menlo Park, California

The *Investigations* curriculum was developed at TERC (formerly Technical Education Research Centers) in collaboration with Kent State University and the State University of New York at Buffalo. The work was supported in part by National Science Foundation Grant No. ESI-9050210. TERC is a nonprofit company working to improve mathematics and science education. TERC is located at 2067 Massachusetts Avenue, Cambridge, MA 02140.

 This project was supported, in part, by the
National Science Foundation
Opinions expressed are those of the authors and not necessarily those of the Foundation

Managing Editor: Catherine Anderson
Series Editor: Beverly Cory
Manuscript Editor: Karen Becker
ESL Consultant: Nancy Sokol Green
Production/Manufacturing Director: Janet Yearian
Production/Manufacturing Coordinator: Joe Conte
Design Manager: Jeff Kelly
Design: Don Taka
Illustrations: Hollis Burkhart, Barbara Epstein-Eagle
Composition: Archetype Book Composition

This book is published by Dale Seymour Publications®, an imprint of Addison Wesley Longman, Inc.

Dale Seymour Publications
2725 Sand Hill Road
Menlo Park, CA 94025
Customer Service: 800-872-1100

 **DALE SEYMOUR PUBLICATIONS®**

Order number DS47005
ISBN 1-57232-758-8
1 2 3 4 5 6 7 8 9 10-ML-01 00 99 98 97

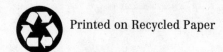 Printed on Recycled Paper

Contents

*Repeated-use sheet

*Repeated-use sheet

Crazy Cakes for Two

Divide each of the "strange cakes" below into two equal halves.
The two halves do not need to have the same shape.

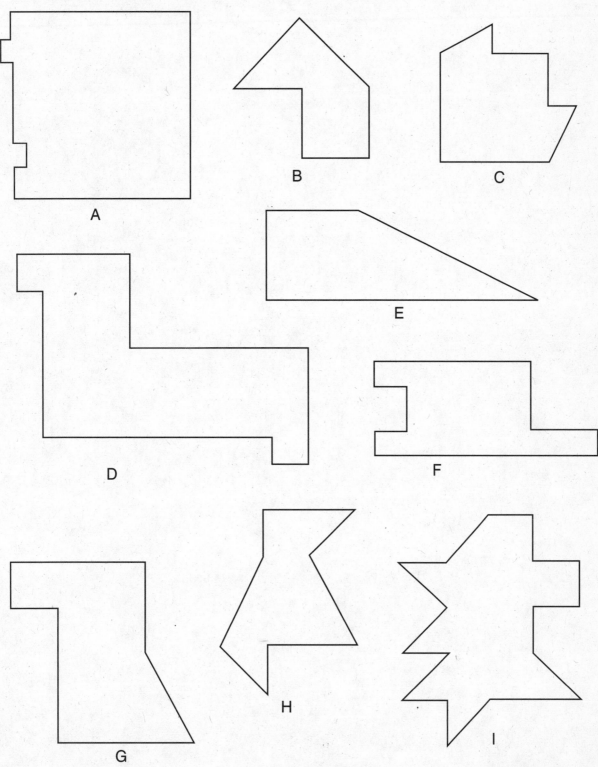

Crazy Cakes for Two

Divide each of the "strange cakes" below into two equal halves.
The two halves do not need to have the same shape.

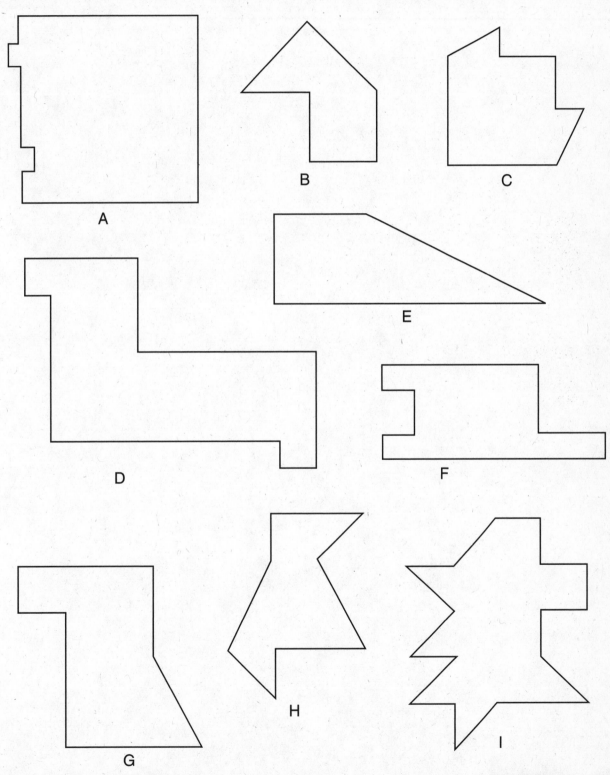

Investigation 1 • Session 1
Different Shapes, Equal Pieces

Dot-Paper Squares

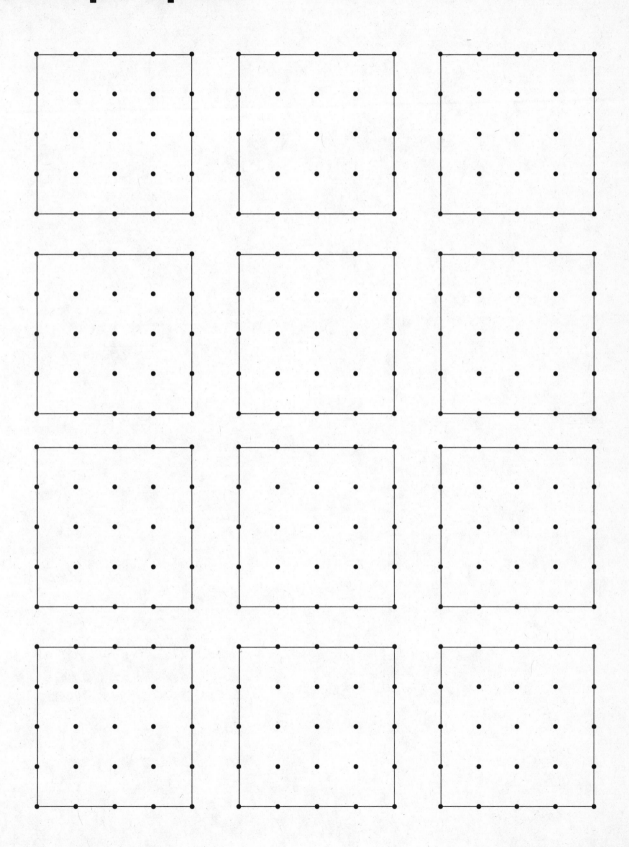

Dot-Paper Squares

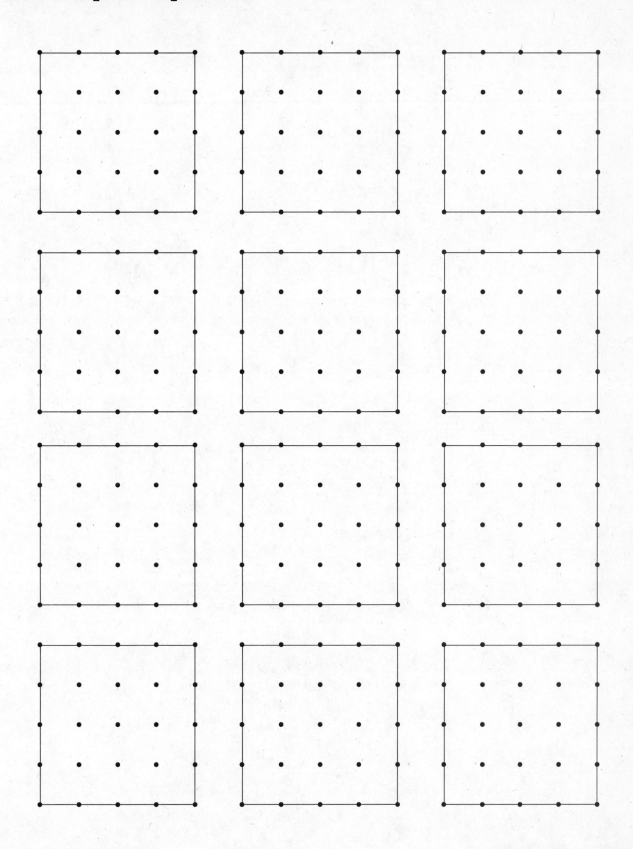

Dot-Paper Squares

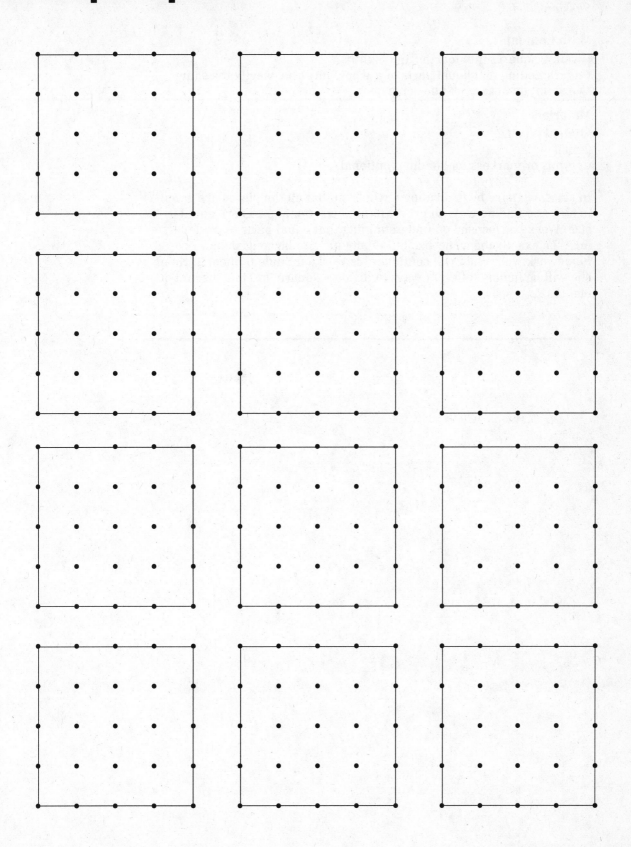

To the Family

Dot-Paper Squares

Sessions 2–4

Math Content

Dividing squares into fourths and eighths
Understanding that equal parts of a whole must be exactly the same
  size but do not have to be congruent

Materials

Student Sheet 2
Pencil
Crayons or markers for shading (optional)

In class, we have been dividing a whole so that all the pieces are equal
in size and finding ways to prove that the fractional parts are equal in
size. Work has focused on understanding that equal parts of a whole
must be exactly the same size but do not have to be congruent. For
homework, your child will continue this work on Student Sheet 2. He or
she will be finding different ways to divide a square into fourths and/or
eighths.

Dot-Paper Squares

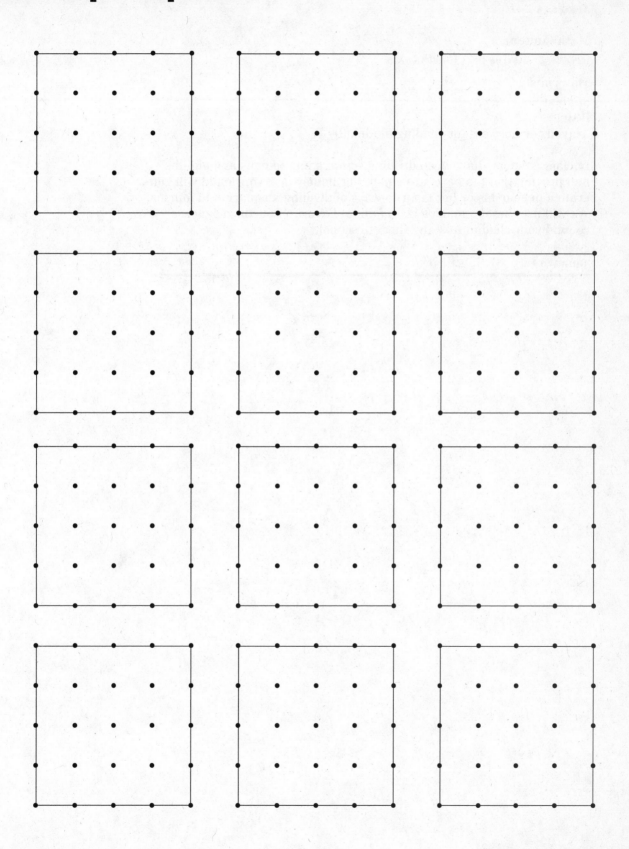

To the Family

Dividing into Fourths

Sessions 2–4

Math Content
Dividing squares into fourths

Materials
Student Sheet 2
Pencil
Crayons or markers for shading (optional)

In class, students have been dividing squares into fourths and eighths and proving that the parts are equal. For homework, your child will generate a page of his or her favorite ways of dividing a square into fourths. We will use these to make a class quilt of Favorite Fourths, so please remind your child to take the sheet to school.

Proving Fractional Parts

1. Prove that this square is divided into halves.

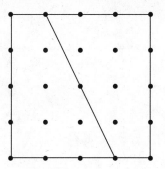

2. Prove that this square is divided into fourths.

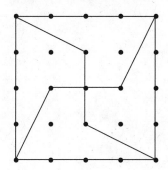

3. Prove that these two shapes have equal area.

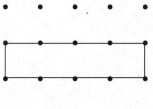 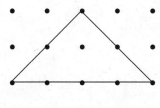

Squares for a Quilt of Fourths

Divide each small square into fourths in a different way.
Use your favorite fourths, or make up new ways of
dividing into fourths. Color each square's fourths right
after you divide it into four parts. Use the same four
colors.

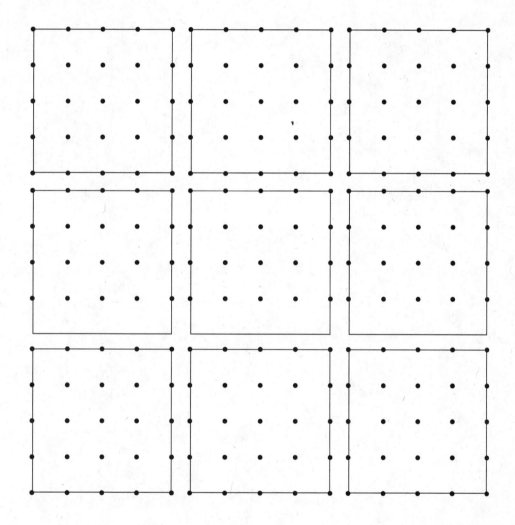

Squares for a Quilt of Fourths

Divide each small square into fourths in a different way.
Use your favorite fourths, or make up new ways of
dividing into fourths. Color each square's fourths right
after you divide it into four parts. Use the same four
colors.

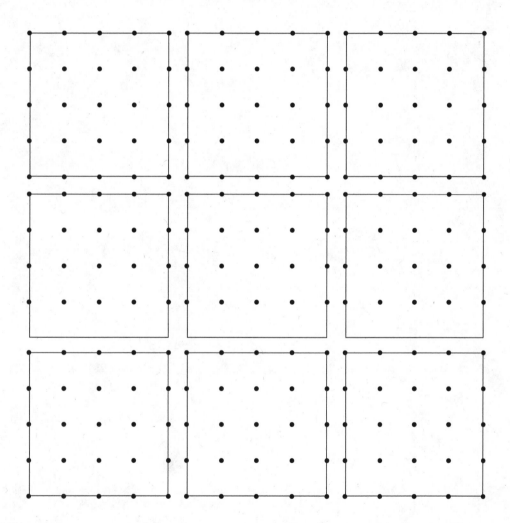

A Favorite Fourth

Draw one of your favorite or most interesting fourths.

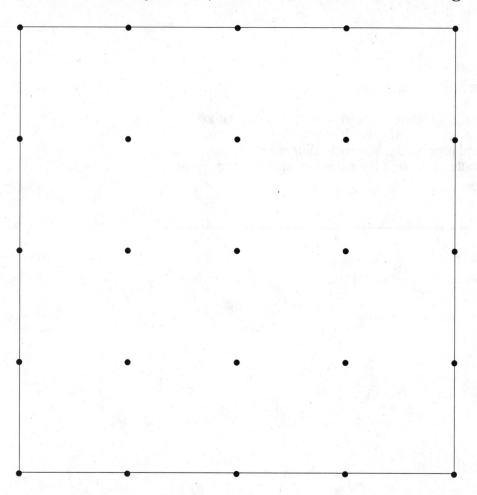

Use diagrams and/or words to prove that this square is divided into fourths. Explain how you know that each piece is one-fourth.

To the Family

A Favorite Fourth

Sessions 2–4

Math Content
Dividing squares into fourths

Materials
Student Sheet 5
Pencil
Crayons or markers for shading (optional)

In class, students have continued to work with fractions, particularly fourths and eighths. For homework, your child will choose a favorite fourth design and record it on Student Sheet 5. Your child will then write about how he or she could prove that the parts are equal fourths, using words and/or diagrams.

Dot-Paper Squares

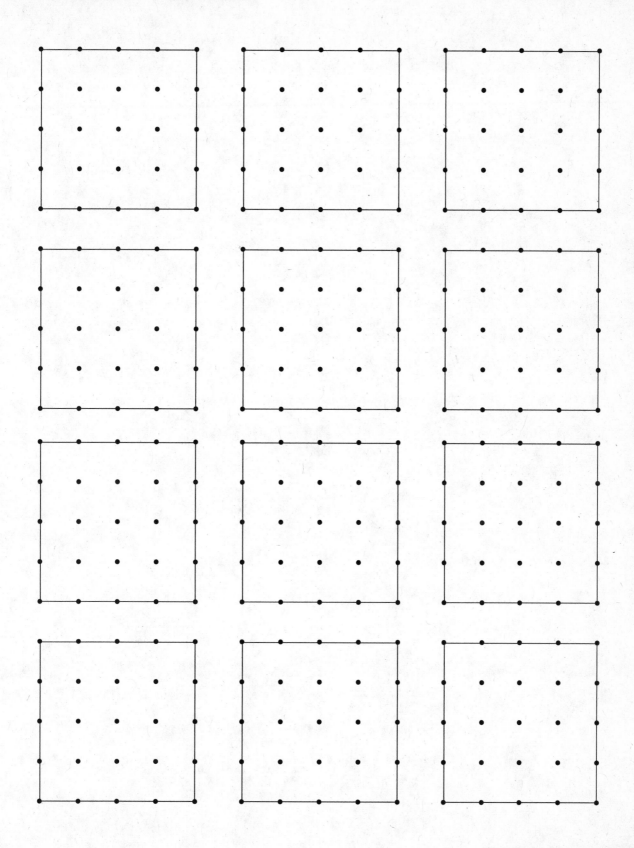

Dot-Paper Squares

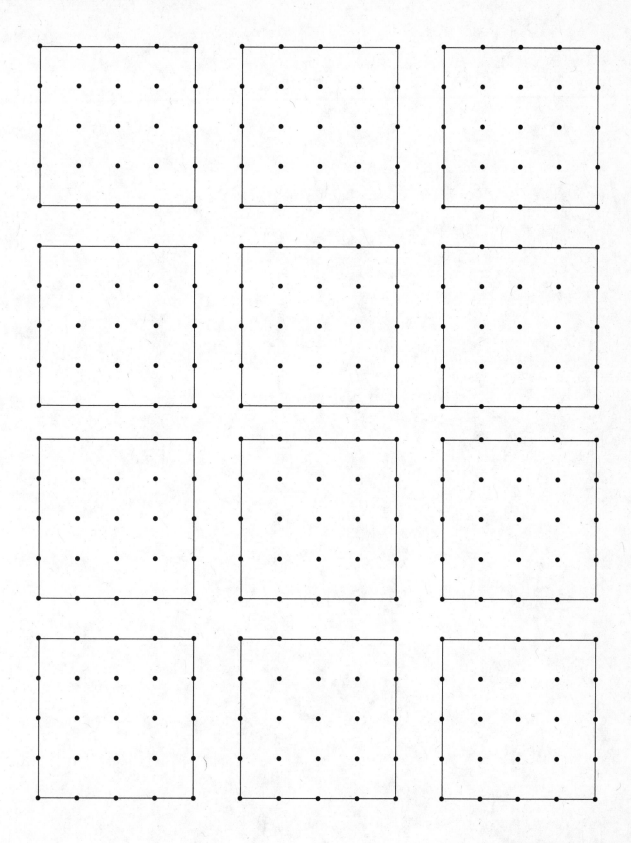

Name Date

Student Sheet 6

Large Dot Square for Combining Fractions

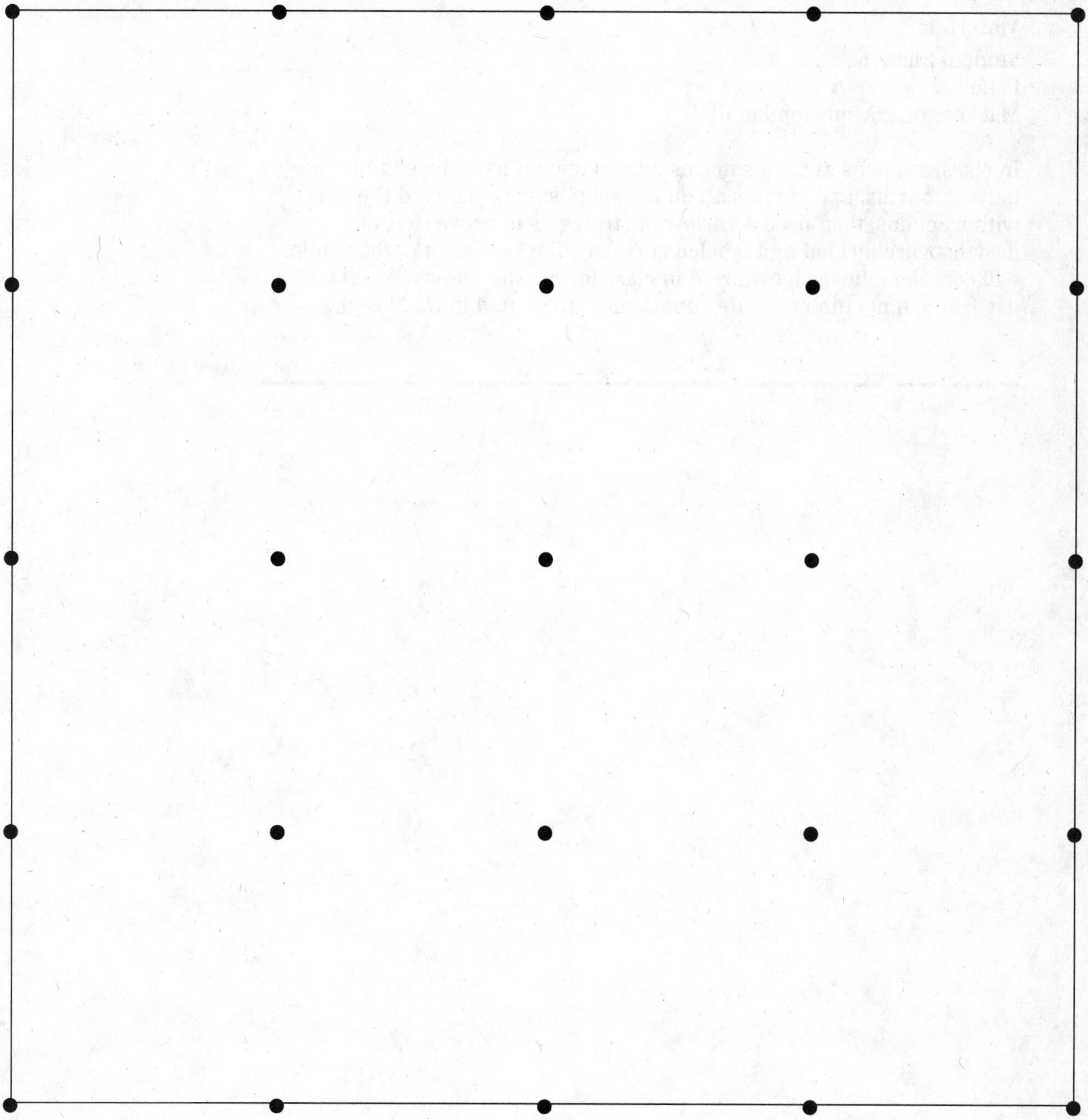

To the Family

Large Dot Square for Combining Fractions

Session 5

Math Content
Using fraction notation to write equations represented in a design

Materials
Student Sheet 6
Pencil
Markers or crayons (optional)

In class, students divided squares into fractional parts by combining halves, fourths, and eighths all on the same square; labeled the parts with fractions; then used a variety of strategies to prove that their designs were divided and labeled correctly. For homework, your child will complete the design started in class (or create a new design) and use fraction notation to write equations represented in the design.

Large Dot Square for Combining Fractions

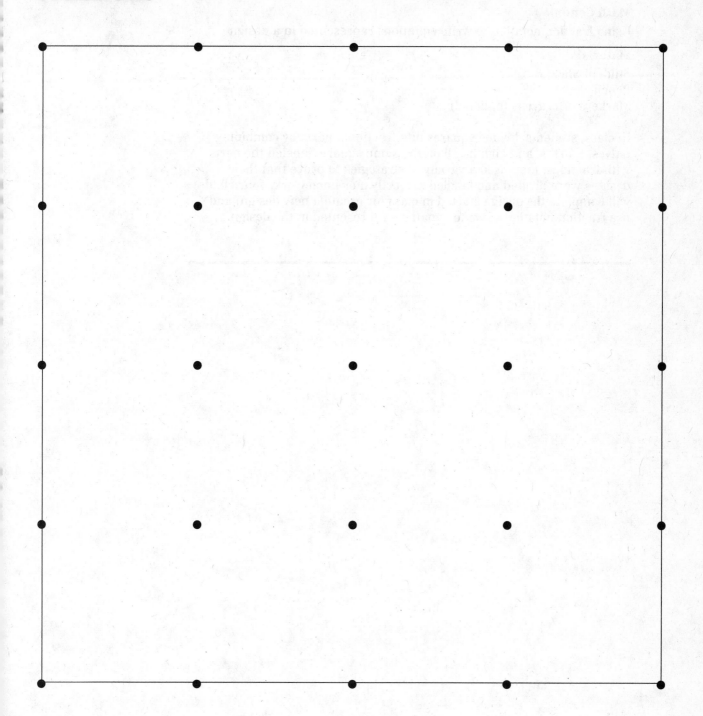

To the Family

Large Dot Square for Combining Fractions

Session 5

Math Content

Using fraction notation to write equations represented in a design

Materials

Student Sheet 6

Pencil

Markers or crayons (optional)

In class, students divided squares into fractional parts by combining halves, fourths, and eighths all on the same square; labeled the parts with fractions; then used a variety of strategies to prove that their designs were divided and labeled correctly. For homework, your child will complete the design started in class (or create a new design) and use fraction notation to write equations represented in the design.

A Dot-Paper Square and Rectangle

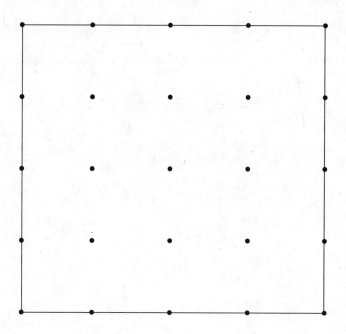

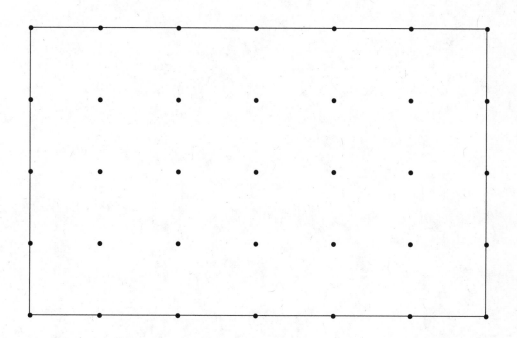

Dot-Paper Rectangles

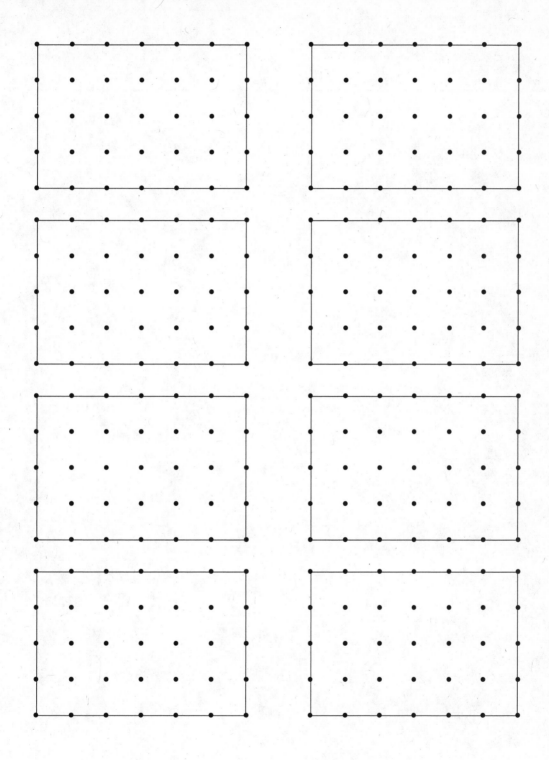

Dot-Paper Rectangles

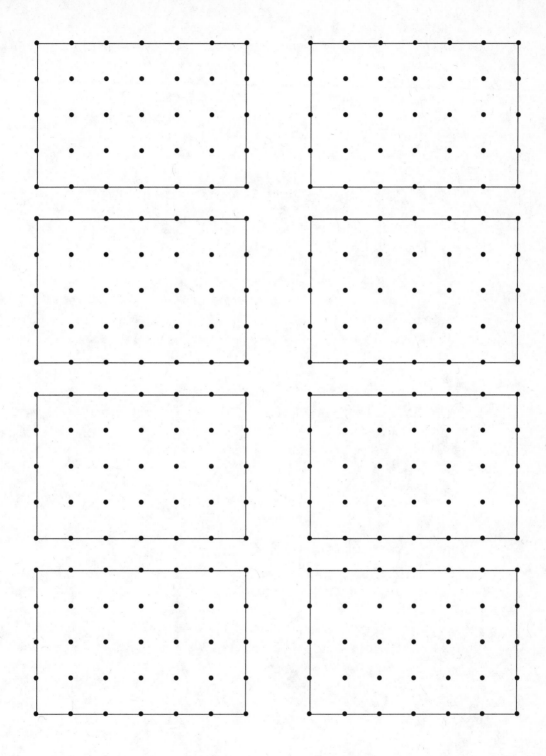

Dot-Paper Rectangles

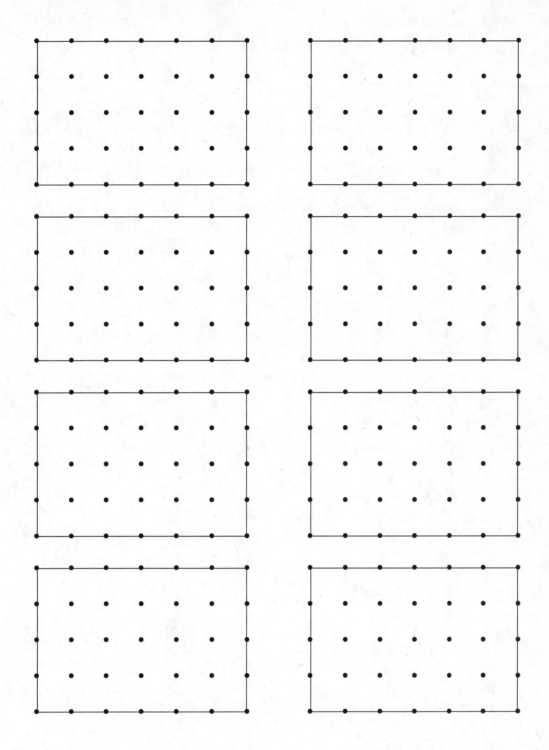

Investigation 2 • Sessions 1–2
Different Shapes, Equal Pieces

Dot-Paper Rectangles

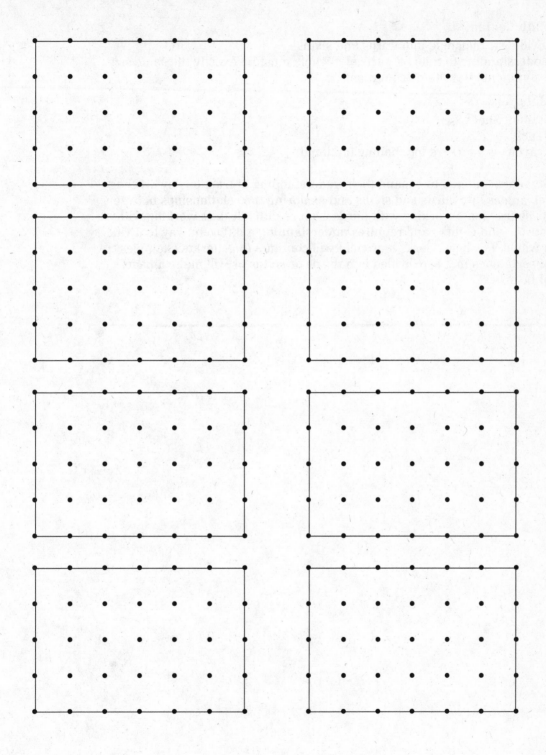

To the Family

Dot-Paper Rectangles

Sessions 1–2

Math Content
Dividing a rectangle into thirds and sixths
Understanding that equal parts of a whole must be exactly the same size but do not have to be congruent

Materials
Student Sheet 8
Pencil
Crayons or markers for shading (optional)

Students continue to expand their understanding of fractions by dividing rectangles into thirds and sixths and exploring the relationships between these fractions. Working with thirds is more difficult than working with fourths and eighths and requires understanding a different way to divide a whole. For homework, your child will continue to generate examples of rectangles that are divided into thirds or sixths or will make a page of favorites.

Thirds and Sixths

Divide this rectangle into thirds (3 equal parts).

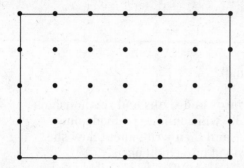

Explain how you know the rectangle is divided into thirds.

_____

Divide this rectangle into sixths (6 equal parts).

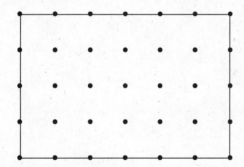

Explain how you know the rectangle is divided into sixths.

To the Family

Thirds and Sixths

Sessions 1–2

Math Content
Dividing a rectangle into thirds and sixths

Materials
Student Sheet 9
Pencil
Crayons or markers for shading (optional)

In class, students continue to explore thirds and sixths and relationships between them. For homework, your child will continue to divide one rectangle into thirds and one into sixths and then write about how she or he knows that the rectangles are divided into equal parts.

Proving Thirds and Sixths

1. Is this rectangle divided into thirds? Explain your answer.

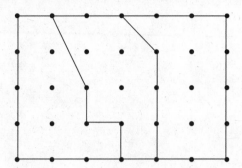

2. a. Is this rectangle divided into sixths? Explain your answer.

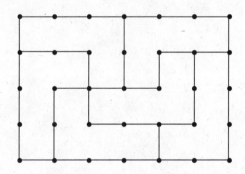

b. Color one-third of the rectangle in 2a.
Explain how you know it is one-third.

3. Some students say $\frac{1}{6}$ is larger than $\frac{1}{4}$
because 6 is larger than 4.
What do you think? Explain.

Dot-Paper Rectangles

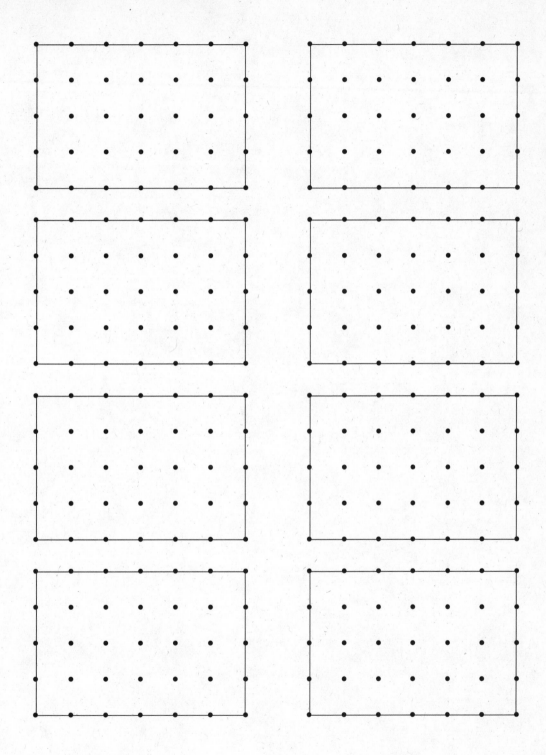

Large Dot Rectangle for Combining Fractions

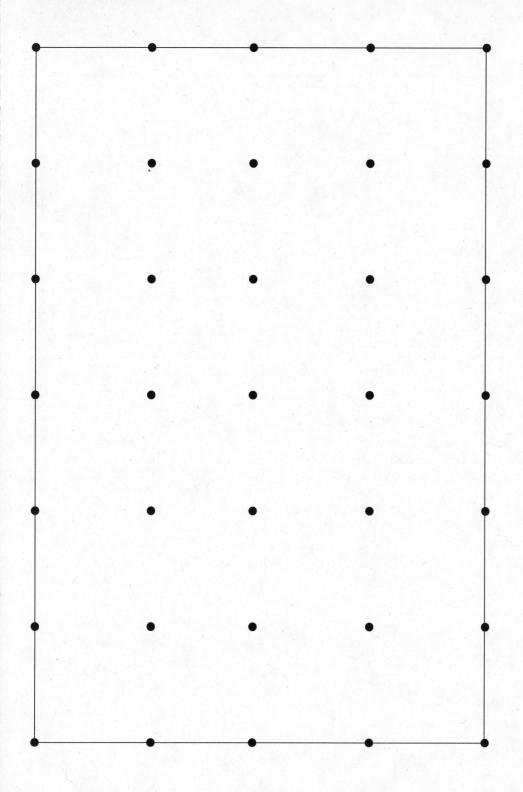

Large Dot Rectangle for Combining Fractions

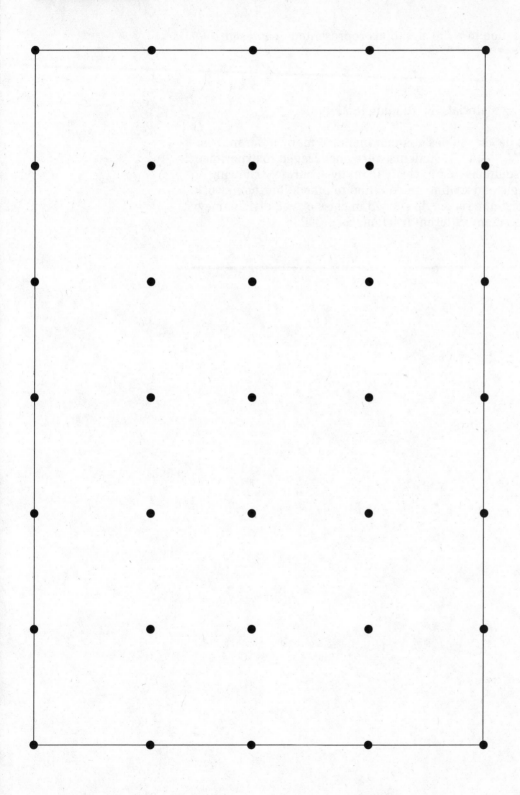

© Dale Seymour Publications®

47

To the Family

Large Dot Rectangle for Combining Fractions

Session 3

Math Content

Using fraction notation to write equations represented in a design

Materials

Student Sheet 11

Pencil

Crayons or coloring materials for shading (optional)

In class, students developed designs that included many different fractions ($\frac{1}{2}$, $\frac{1}{3}$, $\frac{1}{4}$, $\frac{1}{6}$, $\frac{1}{8}$, $\frac{1}{12}$). Students were encouraged to experiment with a variety of solutions and to verify them by accurately showing them on a rectangle and writing an equation to match. For homework, your child will finish the rectangle started in class or will divide a new rectangle, using as many different fractions as possible.

Large Dot Rectangle for Combining Fractions

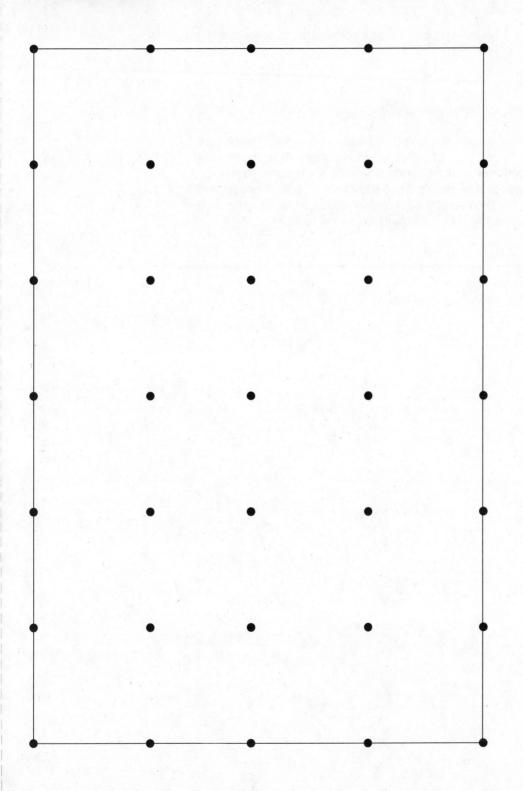

To the Family

Large Dot Rectangle for Combining Fractions
Session 3

Math Content
Using fraction notation to write equations represented in a design

Materials
Student Sheet 11
Pencil
Crayons or coloring materials for shading (optional)

In class, students developed designs that included many different fractions ($1/2$, $1/3$, $1/4$, $1/6$, $1/8$, $1/12$). Students were encouraged to experiment with a variety of solutions, and to verify them by accurately showing them on a rectangle and writing an equation to match. For homework, your child will finish the rectangle started in class or will divide a new rectangle, using as many different fractions as possible.

Blank Square (page 1 of 2)

Marked in Sixths

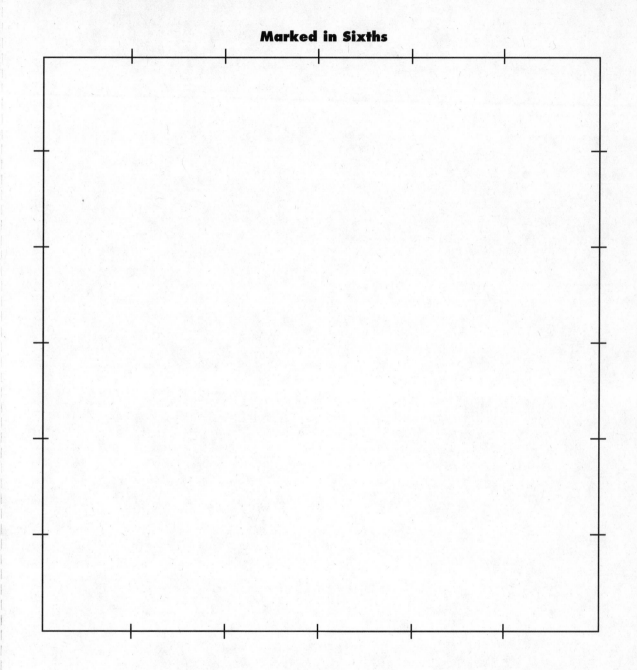

Blank Square (page 2 of 2)

Marked in Eighths

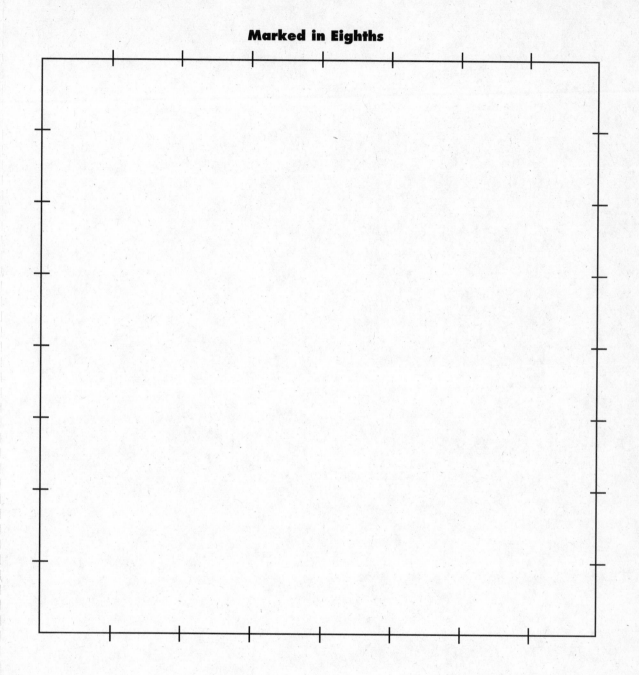

Blank Square (page 1 of 2)

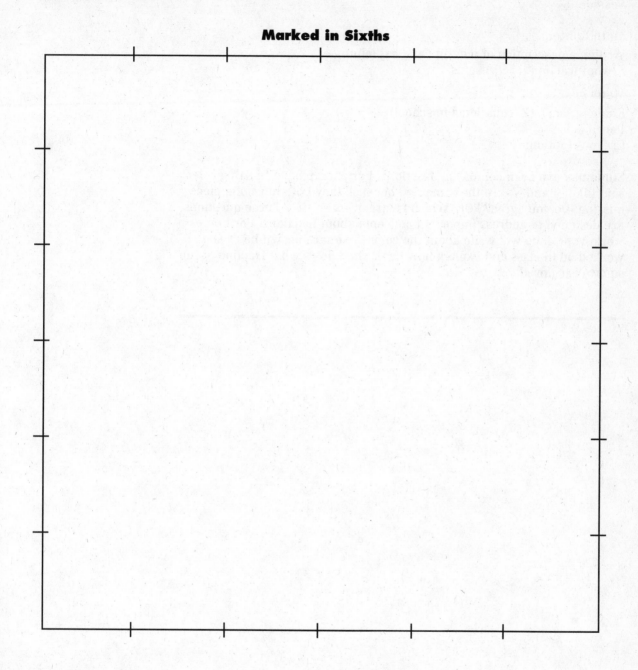

Marked in Sixths

To the Family

Writing About a Colored-Square Design

Session 4

Math Content

Writing a description of a design and explaining
what fraction it represents

Materials

Student Sheet 12 (completed in school)
Pencil
Crayons (optional)

Students have been comparing fractions. For example, "A fourth grader said that 3/4 and 5/6 are the same size because they both have one piece missing. Do you agree?" Or "Which is larger, 2/3 or 3/2?" These questions are designed to address important concepts about fractions. For homework, your child will write about the colored-square design he or she worked on in class and explain how he or she knows what fraction of the square is colored.

Blank Square (page 2 of 2)

Marked in Eighths

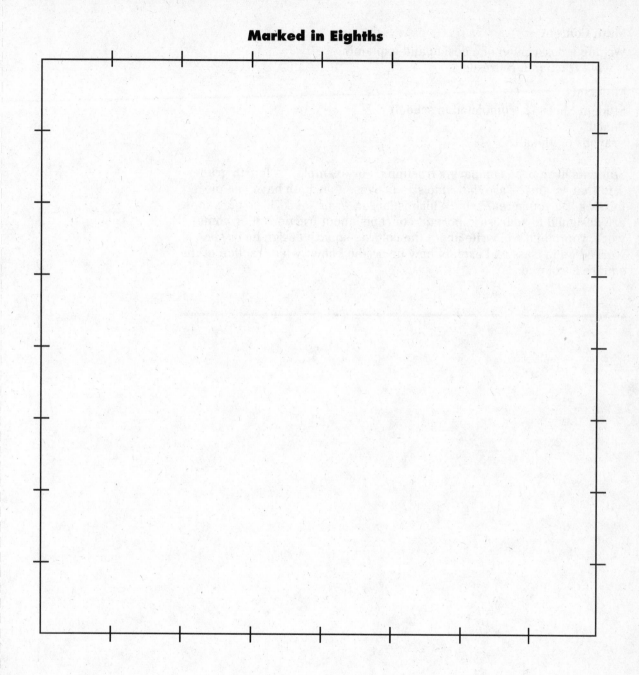

To the Family

Writing About a Colored-Square Design

Session 4

Math Content
Writing a description of a design and explaining
what fraction it represents

Materials
Student Sheet 12 (completed in school)
Pencil
Crayons (optional)

Students have been comparing fractions. For example, "A fourth grader said that 3/4 and 5/6 are the same size because they both have one piece missing. Do you agree?" Or "Which is larger, 2/3 or 3/2?" These questions are designed to address important concepts about fractions. For homework, your child will write about the colored-square design he or she worked on in class and explain how he or she knows what fraction of the square is colored.

Agree or Disagree?

1. A fourth grader said that $\frac{3}{4}$ and $\frac{5}{6}$ are the same size because they both have one piece missing.
   Do you agree? Explain. Use pictures to make your argument clearer.

2. About how big is $\frac{4}{5}$ of this rectangle?
   Show your answer by shading in the rectangle.

   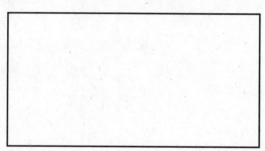

   What other fractions are near $\frac{4}{5}$ in size?

3. Which is larger, $\frac{2}{3}$ or $\frac{3}{2}$?
   Use words and pictures to explain your answer.

$\frac{8}{4}$	$\frac{4}{2}$	$\frac{12}{12}$	$\frac{5}{3}$	$\frac{6}{3}$	$\frac{5}{8}$
$\frac{9}{4}$	$\frac{9}{6}$	$2\frac{1}{2}$	$\frac{10}{8}$	$1\frac{1}{3}$	$1\frac{3}{4}$
$1\frac{1}{2}$	$\frac{8}{3}$	$\frac{5}{2}$	$\frac{0}{2}$	$1\frac{2}{3}$	$\frac{2}{5}$
$\frac{3}{8}$	$\frac{0}{4}$	$\frac{7}{4}$	$\frac{4}{10}$	$\frac{8}{8}$	$\frac{0}{3}$
$\frac{4}{5}$	$\frac{4}{8}$	$\frac{4}{12}$	$\frac{5}{4}$	$\frac{6}{12}$	$\frac{1}{8}$
$\frac{0}{12}$	$\frac{6}{8}$	$\frac{6}{9}$	$\frac{2}{12}$	$\frac{8}{12}$	$\frac{2}{8}$
$\frac{7}{8}$	$1\frac{1}{4}$	$\frac{3}{12}$	$\frac{9}{12}$	$\frac{1}{2}$	$\frac{2}{3}$
$\frac{2}{4}$	$\frac{1}{6}$	$\frac{5}{6}$	$\frac{2}{2}$	$\frac{3}{3}$	$\frac{3}{4}$
$\frac{2}{6}$	$\frac{6}{6}$	$\frac{3}{2}$	$\frac{4}{3}$	$\frac{4}{4}$	$\frac{3}{6}$
$\frac{8}{6}$	$\frac{1}{3}$	$\frac{1}{4}$	$\frac{6}{4}$	$\frac{4}{6}$	$\frac{1}{5}$

Investigation 3 • Resource
Different Shapes, Equal Pieces

BLANK WHOLES FOR FRACTION CARDS

BLANK WHOLES FOR FRACTION CARDS

Materials

Deck of Fraction Cards

Players: 2 or more

How to Play

1. Deal out 7 fraction cards to each player. The remaining fraction cards are placed in a deck in the center of the table.

2. Play proceeds around the circle. The object is to get cards from other players by matching a fraction card in their hands with one in your hand. Cards match if they are equivalent fractions (stand for the same amount). So, $\frac{2}{4}$ matches $\frac{1}{2}$, and $\frac{2}{3}$ matches $\frac{4}{6}$.

3. Each player in turn asks another player if he or she has an equivalent for a fraction, for example, $\frac{2}{4}$. If the second player has any fraction card worth the same amount, the first player gets that card and puts both cards in a "captured fish" pile. If the second player has more than one matching card, the first player gets all of them. If the second player has no matching cards, the first player has to "Fish!"—pick the top card in the face-down pile and add it to his or her hand. If this card results in a match, the player can, on the next turn, put the matching cards in the "captured fish" pile. In addition, the player may ask another player for a different match.

4. The game ends when a player has no more cards or when there are no more matches. In either case, the winner is the person with the most cards in his or her "captured fish" pile.

To the Family

Playing Fraction Fish

Sessions 1–2

Math Content
Comparing fractions
Recognizing equivalent fractions

Materials
How to Play Fraction Fish
Fraction cards for playing Fraction Fish (to be cut apart into a deck)
Scissors
Envelope or plastic bags to hold cards (optional)

In class, students made decks of fraction cards. They drew pictures of
each fraction and used fraction notation to label the cards. Students
used the cards to find and describe fractions that were equivalent to one
another and to play the game Fraction Fish. For homework, your child
will make a simple deck of fraction cards and teach Fraction Fish to
someone at home and then play a few rounds. You might remind your
child to store the fraction cards in a safe place as they will be needed for
another homework assignment in this unit.

Use the fractions below to play Fraction Fish with someone at home. Cut the squares out and use them as cards.

$\frac{2}{3}$	$\frac{1}{6}$	$\frac{4}{2}$	$\frac{6}{6}$	$\frac{0}{2}$
$\frac{1}{4}$	$\frac{3}{6}$	$\frac{9}{6}$	$\frac{1}{8}$	$\frac{2}{4}$
1	$1\frac{1}{2}$	$\frac{4}{6}$	$\frac{6}{8}$	$\frac{0}{4}$
$\frac{4}{8}$	$\frac{8}{8}$	$\frac{8}{4}$	$\frac{6}{4}$	$\frac{4}{4}$
$\frac{6}{12}$	$\frac{0}{6}$	$\frac{1}{2}$	2	$\frac{3}{4}$

Investigation 3 • Resource
Different Shapes, Equal Pieces

Fractions in Containers

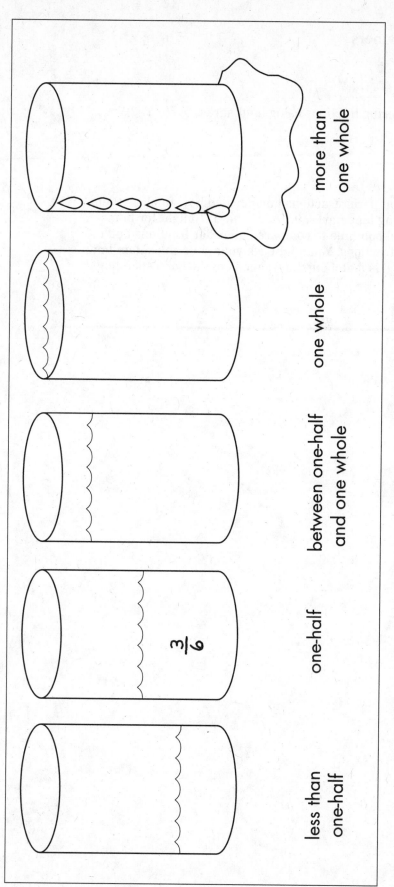

less than
one-half

one-half

$\frac{3}{6}$

between one-half
and one whole

one whole

more than
one whole

Write each fraction in the container in which it belongs.

Cross out each fraction as you use it. ($\frac{3}{6}$ has been done for you.)

There are five fractions for each container.

$\cancel{\frac{3}{6}}$ $\frac{5}{5}$ $\frac{1}{4}$ $\frac{2}{3}$ $\frac{5}{2}$ $\frac{2}{5}$ $\frac{2}{2}$ $\frac{3}{5}$ $\frac{5}{7}$ $\frac{6}{3}$ $\frac{2}{5}$ $\frac{3}{4}$ $\frac{3}{3}$ $\frac{10}{20}$ $\frac{10}{5}$ $\frac{3}{10}$ $\frac{2}{6}$ $\frac{3}{2}$ $\frac{9}{10}$ $\frac{6}{5}$ $\frac{10}{10}$ $\frac{4}{8}$ $\frac{4}{5}$ $\frac{8}{8}$ $\frac{6}{12}$

To the Family

Fractions in Containers

Session 3

Math Content
Comparing and ordering fractions using landmarks (0, 1/2, 1, 2)

Materials
Student Sheet 14
Pencil

In class, students compared fractions and decided how to place them between the following landmarks: 0, 1/2, 1, and 2. Tonight for homework, your child will continue to compare and order fractions and to look for equivalent fractions. You might ask your child to explain how and/or why she or he is matching the fractions to the corresponding container.

Materials

Deck of Fractions Cards

Players: 2 or more

How to Play

1. Divide the deck into equal-sized piles, one for each player. Players hold their piles upside down.

2. In each round, each player turns over the top card in his or her pile. The person with the largest fraction wins, takes the other players' cards, and puts them on the bottom of his or her own pile.

3. If two of the cards show equivalent fractions, those two players turn over another card. Whoever has the larger fraction wins all the other players' cards.

4. The person with the most cards wins. The game can be stopped at any time.

To the Family

Capture Fractions

Sessions 4–5

Math Content
Comparing fractions to see which is larger

Materials
How to Play Capture Fractions
Deck of fraction cards (from Sessions 1–2)

In class, students used their class sets of fraction cards to play Capture Fractions, a game similar to the card game War. The largest fraction in each round wins. For homework, your child will use her or his at-home deck of fraction cards to play Capture Fractions with someone at home. The players should share their thinking—how is each player deciding which is the larger fraction?

Comparing Fractions

1. Circle the larger fraction in each pair.
   Write = if you think they are the same size.
   Next to each pair, show or write about how you decided.

   a. $\dfrac{3}{8}$ $\dfrac{1}{2}$

   b. $\dfrac{2}{3}$ $\dfrac{5}{6}$

   c. $\dfrac{3}{4}$ $\dfrac{4}{3}$

2. Put these fractions in order from smallest to largest.
   Use the clothesline below to order them.

   $\dfrac{1}{2}$ $\dfrac{3}{8}$ $\dfrac{9}{5}$ $\dfrac{1}{6}$ $\dfrac{3}{2}$

   0

How to Play 101 to 200 Bingo

Materials
- 101 to 200 Bingo Board
- One deck of Numeral Cards
- One deck of Tens Cards
- Colored pencil, crayon, or marker

Players: 2 or 3

How to Play

1. Each player takes a 1 from the Numeral Card deck and keeps this card throughout the game.

2. Shuffle the two decks of cards. Place each deck face down on the table.

3. Players use just one Bingo Board. You will take turns and work together to get a Bingo.

4. To determine a play, draw two Numeral Cards and one Tens Card. Arrange the 1 and the two other numerals to make a number between 100 and 199. Then add or subtract the number on your Tens Card. Circle the resulting number on the 101 to 200 Bingo Board.

5. Wild Cards in the Numeral Card deck can be used for any numeral from 0 through 9. Wild Cards in the Tens Card deck can be used as + or – any multiple of 10 from 10 through 70.

6. Some combinations cannot land on the 101 to 200 Bingo Board at all. Make up your own rules about what to do when this happens. (For example, a player could take another turn, or the Tens Card could be *either* added or subtracted in this instance.)

7. The goal is for the players together to circle five adjacent numbers in a row, in a column, or on a diagonal. Five circled numbers is a Bingo.

101	102	103	104	105	106	107	108	109	110
111	112	113	114	115	116	117	118	119	120
121	122	123	124	125	126	127	128	129	130
131	132	133	134	135	136	137	138	139	140
141	142	143	144	145	146	147	148	149	150
151	152	153	154	155	156	157	158	159	160
161	162	163	164	165	166	167	168	169	170
171	172	173	174	175	176	177	178	179	180
181	182	183	184	185	186	187	188	189	190
191	192	193	194	195	196	197	198	199	200

Practice Page
Different Shapes, Equal Pieces

101	102	103	104	105	106	107	108	109	110
111	112	113	114	115	116	117	118	119	120
121	122	123	124	125	126	127	128	129	130
131	132	133	134	135	136	137	138	139	140
141	142	143	144	145	146	147	148	149	150
151	152	153	154	155	156	157	158	159	160
161	162	163	164	165	166	167	168	169	170
171	172	173	174	175	176	177	178	179	180
181	182	183	184	185	186	187	188	189	190
191	192	193	194	195	196	197	198	199	200

Practice Page
Different Shapes, Equal Pieces

0	0	1	1
0	0	1	1
2	2	3	3
2	2	3	3

Practice Page
Different Shapes, Equal Pieces

4	4	5	5
4	4	5	5
<u>6</u>	<u>6</u>	7	7
<u>6</u>	<u>6</u>	7	7

Practice Page
Different Shapes, Equal Pieces

8	8	<u>9</u>	<u>9</u>
8	8	<u>9</u>	<u>9</u>
WILD CARD	**WILD CARD**		
WILD CARD	**WILD CARD**		

Practice Page
Different Shapes, Equal Pieces

+10	+10	+10	+10
+20	+20	+20	+20
+30	+30	+30	+40
+40	+50	+50	+60
+70	**WILD CARD**	**WILD CARD**	**WILD CARD**

Practice Page
Different Shapes, Equal Pieces

-10	-10	-10	-10
-20	-20	-20	-20
-30	-30	-30	-40
-40	-50	-50	-60
-70	**WILD CARD**	**WILD CARD**	**WILD CARD**

Practice Page
Different Shapes, Equal Pieces

Practice Page A

Find the total amount of money in two different ways.

      6 quarters
      6 nickels
      6 pennies
      6 dimes

Here is the first way I found the total amount of money:

Here is the second way I found the total amount of money:

Practice Page B

Find the total amount of money in two different ways.

> 3 quarters
> 9 pennies
> 5 nickels
> 4 dimes

Here is the first way I found the total amount of money:

Here is the second way I found the total amount of money:

Practice Page C

Find the total amount of money in two different ways.

     3 half dollars
     3 pennies
     7 nickels
     5 dimes

Here is the first way I found the total amount of money:

Here is the second way I found the total amount of money:

97

Practice Page D

For each problem, show how you found your solution.

1. There are 18 family members going on a picnic at the park in various cars. Each car holds 5 people. How many cars will be needed?

2. Five family members are making sandwiches for the picnic. How many should each one make to feed the 18 who are going?

3. The 18 family members who are going to the picnic want to drink lemonade. The group takes along five pitchers of lemonade. How many people should each pitcher be able to serve?

Practice Page E

For each problem, show how you found your solution.

1. The office in my school has a phone directory sheet with 3 columns of 46 names in each column. How many names are there on that sheet?

2. There were 46 children in each of three areas in Sol's camp this summer. How many children were at the camp?

3. Molly is planning an activity. She asked me to arrange 3 piles of toothpicks, with 46 in each pile. How many toothpicks will I need?

Practice Page F

For each problem, show how you found your solution.

1. My teacher recycles her newspapers. She can fit 5 days of newspapers into one bag. How many bags will she need for 31 days?

2. How many bags will my teacher need to recycle her newspapers of 40 days?

3. How many bags will my teacher need to recycle her newspapers of 71 days?